D0026930

# Lewis Carroll's
# Games and Puzzles

NEWLY COMPILED AND EDITED BY
## Edward Wakeling

FOREWORD BY
### The Earl of Stockton

DOVER PUBLICATIONS, INC., NEW YORK
*in association with the*
LEWIS CARROLL BIRTHPLACE TRUST,
DARESBURY, CHESHIRE, ENGLAND

Copyright © 1992 by the Lewis Carroll Birthplace Trust.
All rights reserved under Pan American and International
Copyright Conventions.

Published in Canada by General Publishing Company, Ltd.,
30 Lesmill Road, Don Mills, Toronto, Ontario.
Distributed in the United Kingdom by Constable and
Company, Ltd., 3 The Lanchesters, 162–164 Fulham Palace
Road, London W6 9ER.

*Lewis Carroll's Games and Puzzles* is a new work, first published in
1992 by Dover Publications, Inc., New York, in association with
the Lewis Carroll Birthplace Trust, Daresbury, Cheshire,
England (registered office: Coombe Bank Cottage, Snatt's
Road, Uckfield, East Sussex TN22 2AN, England).

Manufactured in the United States of America
Dover Publications, Inc., 31 East 2nd Street, Mineola, N.Y.
11501

*Library of Congress Cataloging-in-Publication Data*

Carroll, Lewis, 1832–1898.
    [Games and puzzles]
    Lewis Carroll's Games and puzzles / newly compiled
and edited by Edward Wakeling; foreword by the Earl of
Stockton.
        p.    cm.
    Includes bibliographical references.
    ISBN 0-486-26922-1
    1. Mathematical recreations.  I. Wakeling, Edward.
II. Title.
QA95.C33 1992
793.7'4—dc20                                                    91-33097
                                                                      CIP

# *Foreword*

## BY THE EARL OF STOCKTON

*Lewis Carroll's Games and Puzzles* is a remarkable and diverting collection of some of the mathematical conundrums produced by one of the more original minds of the nineteenth century: Lewis Carroll.

Edited by Edward Wakeling, a Trustee of the Lewis Carroll Birthplace Trust, who is himself an original and perceptive mathematician, the book adds a new perspective on Lewis Carroll, whose most celebrated book, *Alice's Adventures in Wonderland*, was first published by my great-great-grandfather 125 years ago, followed shortly by its sequel, *Through the Looking-Glass*; both books have remained in print continuously ever since.

I am pleased that Dover Publications have agreed to publish this book in association with the Lewis Carroll Birthplace Trust of Daresbury, in the County of Cheshire, England, which seeks to commemorate this remarkable man's life and works in the place of his birth.

As Chairman of the Trust I have the honour to be Chairman of the advisory committee of the Lewis Carroll Foundation in the United States, and urge all readers to support the setting up of the Lewis Carroll Centre in Daresbury. Thanks to the registered status of the two bodies, all contributions are tax-deductible on both sides of the Atlantic.

STOCKTON.

The Rt. Hon. The Earl of Stockton
Lewis Carroll Birthplace Trust
Coombe Bank Cottage
Snatt's Road
Uckfield
East Sussex TN22 2AN
England

Lewis Carroll Foundation
P.O. Box 275
Roslyn,
Long Island, NY 11576
U.S.A.

# Acknowledgments

Extracts from letters and unpublished papers and diary entries have been made by the kind permission of the C.L. Dodgson Estate. In particular, I record my grateful thanks to Philip Dodgson Jaques, Esq., Senior Trustee of the Estate, for his support in this project.

My thanks also go to Dr. Francis V. Price for allowing me to use papers from his family archive.

I am grateful to Mark Richards, past Chairman of the Lewis Carroll Society, for checking the contents of the problems and their solutions given in this book.

# Contents

## *The Solutions to the Puzzles*

# Introduction

Did you know that Lewis Carroll was a mathematician? He taught mathematics at Oxford University. His real name was Charles Lutwidge Dodgson and for many years he was the mathematical lecturer at Christ Church, Oxford. He wrote *Alice's Adventures in Wonderland* and *Through the Looking-Glass* for Alice Pleasance Liddell, the daughter of the Dean of Christ Church. Both books contain mathematical ideas and problems.

He wrote many other books, including mathematical textbooks for the undergraduates at Oxford and books about his mathematical discoveries. He also wrote two other stories for children. They were not about Alice but about two characters called Sylvie and Bruno. He published several books of poetry and two books about logic. Near the end of his life he worked on a book of mathematical puzzles and games but he died before it could be completed.

This book contains many of the mathematical and logical problems that Lewis Carroll would have included in his edition of puzzles. Some have never before been published. They have remained hidden among his papers and in letters and circulars to his friends. He often sent puzzles to his friends to see if they could solve them. Fortunately, his friends and their families kept these puzzles, so we have many examples of puzzles that he circulated. Quite probably, some of the puzzles were variations of well-known problems of the day, but most were of his own invention.

I hope you enjoy working them out. Hints are given for some problems, and solutions are provided at the end of the book. I have also added a few extra questions for you to attempt, and suggested some investigations which you might like to try.

EDWARD WAKELING

# The Games and Puzzles

— 1 —

# Cakes in a Row

"A barrowful of *what?*" thought Alice. But she had not long to doubt, for the next moment a shower of little pebbles came rattling in at the window, and some of them hit her in the face. "I'll put a stop to this," she said to herself, and shouted out "You'd better not do that again!" which produced another dead silence.

Alice noticed, with some surprise, that the pebbles were all turning into little cakes as they lay on the floor, and a bright idea came into her head.

Here are two rows of five little cakes (or pebbles), equally spaced in each row. Rearrange the cakes to make five rows with four cakes in each row. You may only move *four* of the cakes from their present position.

*Hints:*

1. He was thoughtful and grave—but the orders he gave
     Were enough to bewilder a crew.
   When he cried, "Steer to starboard, but keep her head
       larboard!"
   What on earth was the helmsman to do?

   *The Hunting of the Snark.*

2. Each cake may appear in more than one row.

There is more than one solution to this problem. See if you can find other solutions.

## — 2 —

# More Cakes in a Row

"If I eat one of these cakes," she thought, "it's sure to make *some* change in my size; and, as it ca'n't possibly make me larger, it must make me smaller, I suppose."

Before Alice swallowed one of the cakes, she tried some other problems about arranging the cakes in rows.

1. Her first problem was to put nine cakes into eight rows with three cakes in each row.

2. Then she tried to put nine cakes into nine rows with three cakes in each row.

3. Finally, with a little thought she managed to put nine cakes into ten rows with three cakes in each row.

See if you can solve these three arrangement problems that Alice succeeded in tackling.

*Hint:*

> You boil it in sawdust: you salt it in glue:
> You condense it with locusts and tape:
> Still keeping one principal object in view——
> To preserve its symmetrical shape.

> *The Hunting of the Snark.*

Make up some of your own arrangement problems like these using counters or bottle tops.

— **3** —

## On the Top of a High Wall

In the summer of 1870, Lewis Carroll wrote to his young friend, Mary Watson. In his letter he included this verse-riddle:

> Dreaming of apples on a wall,
> And dreaming often, dear,
> I dreamed that, if I counted all,
> —How many would appear?

How many apples do you think would appear?

This verse-riddle, together with others that follow, were written for some of his young friends and later published in *Aunt Judy's Magazine* in December 1870. There were seven examples called "Puzzles from Wonderland"; the solutions were published in the next issue, also in verse, but not by Lewis Carroll.

Make up some of your own verse-riddles.

## — 4 —

# A Sticky Problem

Here is the next "Puzzle from Wonderland"; again in verse:

> A stick I found that weighed two pound:
>   I sawed it up one day
> In pieces eight of equal weight!
>   How much did each piece weigh?

Most people say that the answer is four ounces, but this is wrong. Why?

Hardly knowing what she did, she picked up a little bit of stick, and held it out to the puppy: whereupon the puppy jumped into the air off all its feet at once, with a yelp of delight, and rushed at the stick, and made believe to worry it: then Alice dodged behind a great thistle, to keep herself from being run over; and, the moment she appeared on the other side, the puppy made another rush at the stick, and tumbled head over heels in its hurry to get hold of it. . . .

## — 5 —

# Two Brothers and a Box

Here is another verse-riddle from "Puzzles from Wonderland":

> John gave his brother James a box:
> About it there were many locks.
>
> James woke and said it gave him pain;
> So gave it back to John again.
>
> The box was not with lid supplied,
> Yet caused two lids to open wide:
>
> And all these locks had never a key—
> What kind of box, then, could it be?

If you know what kind of box it was that John gave to his brother James, then see if you can write a poem in answer to the question.

# Wise Eyes

This next puzzle was also included in "Puzzles from Wonderland."

When the King found that his money was nearly all gone, and that he really *must* live more economically, he decided on sending away most of his Wise Men. There were some hundreds of them—very fine old men, and magnificently dressed in green velvet gowns with gold buttons: if they *had* a fault, it was that they always contradicted one another when he asked for their advice—and they certainly ate and drank enormously. So, on the whole, he was rather glad to get rid of them. But there was an old law, which he did not dare to disobey, which said that there must always be

"Seven blind of both eyes:
Ten blind of one eye:
Five that see with both eyes:
Nine that see with one eye."

If this be the case, how many wise men could he keep without disobeying the old law?

# Alice's Multiplication Tables

". . . Oh dear, how puzzling it all is! I'll try if I know all the things I used to know. Let me see: four times five is twelve, and four times six is thirteen, and four times seven is—oh dear! I shall never get to twenty at that rate!"

Why couldn't Alice get to twenty at that rate?

*Hint:*

This problem involves different ways of counting; for example, we count weeks using base 7. Ten days becomes one week and three days; 10 is the same as 13 in base 7. 13 means one week and three days remaining. Fifteen days would be two weeks and one day remaining; 15 is the same as 21 in base 7.

If we count in a base larger than ten, we need to invent new symbols for some numbers; 26 is 1T in base 16, where T stands for ten.

Now let us go back to Alice's multiplication tables:

$$4 \times 5 = 12 \qquad \text{(20 but counting in base 18)}$$
$$4 \times 6 = 13 \qquad \text{(24 but counting in base 21)}$$
$$4 \times 7 = \ldots \ldots \qquad \text{(continue the pattern)}$$

If you extend the multiplication tables far enough, you will discover why Alice could not reach an answer of 20.

# Magic Postal Square

"Curiouser and curiouser!" cried Alice (she was so much surprised that for the moment she quite forgot how to speak good English). "Now I'm opening out like the largest telescope that ever was! Good-bye feet!" (for when she looked down at her feet, they seemed to be almost out of sight, they were getting so far off). "Oh, my poor little feet, I wonder who will put on your shoes and stockings for you now, dears? I'm sure I sha'n't be able! I shall be a great deal too far off to trouble myself about you: you must manage the best way you can— but I must be kind to them," thought Alice, "or perhaps they wo'n't walk the way I want to go! Let me see, I'll give them a new pair of boots every Christmas."

And she went on planning to herself how she would manage it. "They must go by the carrier," she thought; "and how funny it'll seem, sending presents to one's own feet! And how odd the directions will look!

> Alice's Right Foot, Esq.
> Hearthrug,
> > near the Fender,
> > > (with Alice's love).

Oh dear, what nonsense I'm talking!"

Lewis Carroll invented a magic-square problem using the postal values of his day. In Victorian times, these were the nine smallest postage values available as stamps:

$$\tfrac{1}{2}d, 1d, 1\tfrac{1}{2}d, 2d, 2\tfrac{1}{2}d, 3d, 3\tfrac{1}{2}d, 4d, 5d$$

By placing postages on the nine squares on the next page, make each row, column and diagonal total to the same amount. You may use ten stamps; that is, one each of the above amounts and one extra from the list. On one square you may place two stamps.

— 9 —

# Who's Telling the Truth?

"What do you mean by that?" said the Caterpillar, sternly. "Explain yourself!"

In Lewis Carroll's diaries, which he kept nearly all his adult life, he occasionally entered puzzles that occurred to him. This is a puzzle based on a piece of logic that appears in his diary.

The Dodo says that the Hatter tells lies.
The Hatter says that the March Hare tells lies.
The March Hare says that both the Dodo and the Hatter tell lies.

Who is telling the truth?

Explain your answer.

*Hint:*

Consider whether each character in turn is telling the truth; you will end up with only one possible solution.

# Lanrick

This is an early version of a game for two players, invented in 1878. Lewis Carroll modified and developed the game before publishing the final version in 1893.

The game is played on a chessboard, each player having five men; the other requisites are a die and dice box, and something (such as a coin) to mark a square. The interior of the board, excluding the border squares, is regarded as containing six rows and six columns. It must be agreed which is the first row and first column.

1. The Players set their men in turn, alternately, on any border-squares they like.

2. The die is thrown twice, and a square marked accordingly, the first throw fixing the row, the second, the column; the marked square, with the eight surrounding squares, forms the first "rendezvous", into which the men are to be played.

3. The men move like chess-queens; in playing for the first "rendezvous", each Player may move over six squares, either with one man, or dividing the move among several.

4. When one Player has got all his men into the "rendezvous" the other must remove from the board one of his men that has failed to get in; the die is then thrown for a new "rendezvous", for which each Player may move over as many squares as he had men in the last "rendezvous", and one more.

5. If it be found that either Player has all his men already in the new "rendezvous", the die must be thrown again, till a "rendezvous" is found where this is not the case.

6. The Game ends when one Player has lost all his men.

Play this game with a friend, and try to work out a strategy that will help you to win.

— 11 —

# *Russian Family*

Lewis Carroll wrote in his diary for June 30, 1892: "Invented what I think is a *new* kind of riddle." The riddle that he had invented concerned a Russian family, and this is the problem:

> A Russian had three sons.
> The first, named Rab, became a lawyer.
> The second, [named] Ymra, became a soldier.
> The third became a sailor: what was his name?

The novelty is in the method of solution. Here is a hint taken from one of Lewis Carroll's other books for children, *Sylvie and Bruno Concluded*, published in 1893.

> Sylvie was arranging some letters on a board—E—V—I—L. "Now, Bruno," she said, "what does that spell?"
> Bruno looked at it, in solemn silence, for a minute. "I know what it *doesn't* spell!" he said at last.
> "That's no good," said Sylvie. "What *does* it spell?"
> Bruno took another look at the mysterious letters. "Why, it's 'LIVE', backwards!" he exclaimed. (I thought it was, indeed.)
> "How *did* you manage to see that?" said Sylvie.
> "I just twiddled my eyes," said Bruno, "and then I saw it directly."

—— **12** ——

# *Fair Shares*

Two brothers were left some money, amounting to an exact number of pounds all in coins, to divide between them. The elder undertook the division.

"But your heap is larger than mine!" cried the younger.

"True," said the elder. "Allow me to present you with one-third of my heap."

The younger added it to his heap, and after looking thoughtfully at the now gigantic pyramid, he suddenly exclaimed "I am well off now! Here is half the heap for you."

"You are generous," said the other, as he swept up the money. "Two-thirds of this heap is the least I can offer you."

"I will not be outdone in generosity!" cried the younger, hastily handing over three-quarters of his property.

"Prudence is a virtue," remarked the elder. "Content yourself with two-thirds of my present wealth."

"One-third of mine is all I can now afford!" retorted the other.

"And now, if I give you one pound," remarked the elder brother, "we shall, I think, be square?"

He was right. How much money was divided between them?

This problem has been very slightly modified so that it applies to present-day currency, the original problem being in pounds, shillings and pence. There is probably more than one solution to the problem. See if you can find the smallest number of pounds that may be divided between the two brothers following the conditions given in this conversation.

—— **13** ——

# A Mysterious Number

The number 142,857 does not at first sight appear to have anything odd about it, yet there are some strange things about it. Let us multiply it by the numbers 2 to 7 and see the result.

> 142,857 by 2 is 285,714
> 142,857 by 3 is 428,571
> 142,857 by 4 is 571,428
> 142,857 by 5 is 714,285
> 142,857 by 6 is 857,142
> 142,857 by 7 is 999,999

The first five products, you will observe, are composed not only of the same figures, but of the same figures in the same order, though beginning with a different figure each time. And the strangest part of it all is that 142,857 multiplied by 7 is 999,999, but after that point the products lose their oddity.

Can you explain this result.

*Hint:* Try working out 1 divided by 7.

Investigate other results like this, such as 1 divided by 9, and 1 divided by 11. See if you can find other mysterious numbers that have similar properties.

## —— 14 ——

# *Looking-Glass Time*

Among some papers that Lewis Carroll sent to his old mathematics tutor, Professor Bartholomew "Bat" Price, were a number of puzzles and problems that have never before been published. These came to light a few years ago.

This one concerns a clock with a special kind of clock face:

> A clock face has all the hours indicated by the same mark, and both hands the same in length and form. It is opposite to a looking-glass. Find the time between 6 and 7 when the time as read direct and in the looking-glass shall be the same.

Lewis Carroll was in the habit of sending sample problems to friends to see if they could find solutions. Sometimes he was surprised to find that eminent mathematical colleagues at Oxford University gave different and contradictory solutions to his problems. Professor Bat Price was a lifelong friend with whom Lewis Carroll often discussed his mathematical discoveries and inventions. He is immortalized by Lewis Carroll in *Alice's Adventures in Wonderland* in these verses:

> Twinkle, twinkle, little bat!
> How I wonder what you're at!
> Up above the world you fly,
> Like a tea-tray in the sky.

Professor Bat Price was renowned for lecturing well above the heads of his students.

## — 15 —

# *Painting Cubes*

Here is another problem that was found among the papers that Lewis Carroll sent to his old mathematics tutor, Professor Bartholomew Price.

Imagine that you have some wooden cubes.

You also have six paint tins each containing a different colour of paint.

You paint a cube using a different colour for each of the six faces.

How many different cubes can be painted using the same set of six colours?

Remember that two cubes are different only when it is not possible, by turning one, to make it correspond with the other.

As a further problem, try to find a way of coding and recording the different cubes.

A large rose-tree stood near the entrance of the garden: the roses growing on it were white, but there were three gardeners at it, busily painting them red. . . .

"Would you tell me please," said Alice, a little timidly, "why you are painting those roses?"

Five and Seven said nothing, but looked at Two. Two began in a low voice, "Why, the fact is, you see, Miss, this here ought to have been a *red* rose-tree, and we put a white one in by mistake; and, if the Queen was to find it out, we should all have our heads cut off, you know."

—— **16** ——

# Going Out

Here is a logical problem (slightly modified) that was found among the papers sent by Lewis Carroll to his old mathematics tutor, Professor Bartholomew Price.

There are six characters in a house:

> Alice (A), a Baby (B), the Cook (C), the Duchess (D), Cheshire Puss (E) and the Frog Footman (F). They are allowed to go out, under certain conditions, which are always to be observed, as follows:
>
> (1) When A, B and C go out, F must stay in;
> (2) When C, D and E go out, F must go out.
>
> It is required to work out whether it is possible, consistently with these rules, for A and B to go out together.

Find a proof that decides whether or not Alice and the Baby can go out of the house together.

> "I shall sit here," the Footman remarked, "till to-morrow——"
>
> At this moment the door of the house opened, and a large plate came skimming out, straight at the Footman's head: it

just grazed his nose, and broke to pieces against one of the trees behind him.

"—or next day, maybe," the Footman continued in the same tone, exactly as if nothing had happened.

"How am I to get in?" asked Alice again, in a louder tone.

"*Are* you to get in at all?" said the Footman. "That's the first question, you know."

It was, no doubt: only Alice did not like to be told so. "It's really dreadful," she muttered to herself, "the way all the creatures argue. It's enough to drive one crazy!"

—— 17 ——

# Four Brothers and a Monkey

Here is another puzzle found among the papers that Lewis Carroll sent to his old mathematics tutor, Professor Bartholomew Price.

There are four brothers sitting at a table with a monkey. On the table is a pile of nuts.

The first brother gives one nut to the monkey, and takes a quarter of the remaining nuts for himself. He gives the rest to the second brother.

The second brother gives one nut to the monkey, and takes a quarter of the remaining nuts for himself. He gives the rest to the third brother.

The third brother gives one nut to the monkey, and takes a quarter of the remaining nuts for himself. He gives the rest to the fourth brother.

The fourth brother gives one nut to the monkey and takes a quarter of the remaining nuts for himself.

The remaining nuts are divided equally between the four brothers.

How many nuts were on the table to start with?

There are many solutions to this problem. Try to find the smallest number of nuts which it is possible to start with fulfilling the statements given above.

# *Two Clocks*

The Hatter was the first to break the silence. "What day of the month is it?" he said, turning to Alice: he had taken his watch out of his pocket, and was looking at it uneasily, shaking it every now and then, and holding it to his ear.

When he was young, Lewis Carroll helped his brothers and sisters write a number of family magazines. In one called *The Rectory Umbrella*, dated around 1850, he included a puzzle titled "Difficulties, Number 2."

> Which is best, a clock that is right only once a year, or a clock that is right twice every day?

Make up your mind before reading on.

Lewis Caroll wrote this in the family magazine for his readers:

> "The latter," you reply, "unquestionably." Very good, reader, now attend.
> I have two clocks: one doesn't go *at all*, and the other loses a minute a day: which would you prefer? "The losing one," you answer, "without a doubt." Now observe: the one which loses a minute a day has to lose twelve hours, or seven hundred and twenty minutes before it is right again, consequently it is only right once in two years, whereas the other is evidently right as often as the time it points to comes round, which happens twice a day.
> So you've contradicted yourself *once.*
> "Ah, but," you say, "what's the use of its being right twice a day, if I ca'n't tell when the time comes?"
> Why, suppose the clock points to eight o'clock, don't you see that the clock is right *at* eight o'clock? Consequently when eight o'clock comes round your clock is right.
> "Yes, I see *that*," you reply.
> Very good, then you've contradicted yourself *twice*: now get out of the difficulty as best you can, and don't contradict yourself again if you can help it.

# Sitting in a Circle

In 1895, Lewis Carroll published a book called *Pillow-Problems*. In it he reproduced 72 problems that he had personally worked out in his head without putting pen to paper. He solved most of them while lying awake at night, hence the title.

This is problem number 8. The amounts of money have been adapted to fit today's currency, but the problem and the method of solution remain unchanged.

> Some men sat in a circle, so that each had two neighbours; and each had a certain number of pounds. The first had one pound more than the second, who had one pound more than the third, and so on. The first gave one pound to the second, who gave two pound to the third, and so on, each giving one pound more than he received, as long as possible. There were then two neighbours, one of whom had four times as much as the other.

[1] How many men were there?

[2] How much had the poorest man at first?

## — 20 —

# *Bags of Counters*

Here are three probability problems from *Pillow-Problems*.

The first is problem number 5:

> A bag contains one counter, known to be either white or black. A white counter is put in, the bag shaken, and a counter drawn out, which proves to be white. What is now the chance of drawing a white counter?

The second is problem number 16:

> There are two bags, one containing a counter, known to be either white or black; the other containing 1 white and 2 black. A white is put into the first, the bag shaken, and a counter drawn out, which proves to be white. Which course will now give the best chance of drawing a white—to draw from one of the two bags without knowing which it is, or to empty one bag into the other and then draw?

Finally, problem number 72:

> A bag contains 2 counters, as to which nothing is known except that each is either black or white. Ascertain their colours without taking them out of the bag.

# Going Round in Circles

See if you can draw these diagrams, tracing them in *one* line each, or, if not, in how many, going by the rule of always crossing to a new circle or oval at every point of contact, and keeping *on*, not turning back.

(1)

(2)

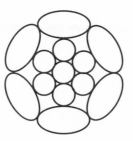

(3)

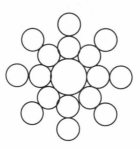

[This problem was found on a sheet dated April 9, 1889.]

# Hidden Names

This poem appears at the end of *Through the Looking-Glass*, which was first published in December 1871. It is called an acrostic poem because it conceals a name, the identity of the real Alice.
Can you find her name?

> A boat, beneath a sunny sky
> Lingering onward dreamily
> In an evening of July—
>
> Children three that nestle near,
> Eager eye and willing ear,
> Pleased a simple tale to hear—
>
> Long has paled that sunny sky:
> Echoes fade and memories die:
> Autumn frosts have slain July.
>
> Still she haunts me, phantomwise,
> Alice moving under skies
> Never seen by waking eyes.
>
> Children yet, the tale to hear,
> Eager eye and willing ear,
> Lovingly shall nestle near.
>
> In a Wonderland they lie,
> Dreaming as the days go by,
> Dreaming as the summers die:
>
> Ever drifting down the stream—
> Lingering in the golden gleam—
> Life, what is it but a dream?

Write an acrostic poem using your own, or a friend's name.

# *Another Hidden Name*

This dedicatory poem appears at the beginning of Lewis Carroll's epic nonsense book, *The Hunting of the Snark*, which was first published in 1876. This acrostic poem hides the name of a child-friend. Her name appears twice; can you find her name in both instances?

> Girt with a boyish garb for boyish task,
>     Eager she wields her spade: yet loves as well
> Rest on a friendly knee, intent to ask
>     The tale he loves to tell.
>
> Rude spirits of the seething outer strife,
>     Unmeet to read her pure and simple spright,
> Deem, if you list, such hours a waste of life
>     Empty of all delight!
>
> Chat on, sweet Maid, and rescue from annoy
>     Hearts that by wiser talks are unbeguiled.
> Ah, happy he who owns that tenderest joy,
>     The heart-love of a child!
>
> Away, fond thoughts, and vex my soul no more!
>     Work claims my wakeful nights, my busy days—
> Albeit bright memories of that sunlit shore
>     Yet haunt my dreaming gaze!

# Well-Hidden Names

This poem appears at the beginning of Lewis Carroll's *Sylvie and Bruno Concluded*, published in 1893. The name of the child to which the book is dedicated is well hidden; see if you can find it.

> Dreams, that elude the Maker's frenzied grasp—
> Hands, stark and still, on a dead Mother's breast,
> Which nevermore shall render clasp for clasp,
> Or deftly soothe a weeping Child to rest—
> In suchlike forms me listeth to portray
> My Tale, here ended. Thou delicious Fay—
> The guardian of a Sprite that lives to tease thee—
> Loving in earnest, chiding but in play
> The merry mocking Bruno! Who, that sees thee,
> Can fail to love thee, Darling, even as I?—
> My sweetest Sylvie, we must say "Good-bye!"

This poem appears at the beginning of Lewis Carroll's *Game of Logic*, published in 1886. Again, the name of the child to which the book is dedicated is well hidden; can you find it?

> I charm in vain: for ever again,
> All keenly as my glance I bend,
>   Will Memory, goddess coy,
>   Embody for my joy
> Departed days, nor let me gaze
>   On thee, my Fairy Friend!
>
> Yet could thy face, in mystic grace,
> A moment smile on me, 'twould send
>   Far-darting rays of light
>   From Heaven athwart the night,
> By which to read in very deed
>   Thy spirit, sweetest Friend!

So may the stream of Life's long dream
Flow gently onward to its end,
   With many a floweret gay,
   A-down its willowy way:
May no sigh vex, no care perplex,
   My loving little Friend!

## — 25 —

# *Handicaps*

"Well, in our country," said Alice, still panting a little, "you'd generally get to somewhere else—if you ran very fast for a long time as we've been doing."

"A slow sort of country!" said the Queen. "Now, here, you see, it takes all the running you can do, to keep in the same place. If you want to get somewhere else, you must run at least twice as fast as that!"

In April 1897, Lewis Carroll wrote a letter to Enid Stevens, and in it he included a puzzle about running a race. One of Enid's friends, Helen Drew, had hoped to visit Lewis Carroll and dine with him, but the invitation had not been settled; the puzzle was compensation until arrangements could be made. The letter said:

Here's an arithmetical puzzle, which I invented 2 days ago, which you can give to Helen, to console her for not coming to dine.

"Three men, A, B, and C, are to run a race of a quarter-of-a-mile. Whenever A runs against B, he loses 10 yards in every 100: whenever B runs against C, he gains 10 yards in every 100. How should they be handicapped?" ("Handicapping" means that the inferior runners are allowed a start: and the amount is so calculated that, if all were to run at their previous rates, it would be a dead heat: i.e. they would all get to the winning post at the same moment.)

What handicap distances should be allowed to runners A and C?

# The Fox, the Goose and the Bag of Corn

In January 1878, Lewis Carroll wrote a letter to Jessie Sinclair, and in it he included a well-known puzzle about a fox, a goose and a bag of corn. The problem was included for Jessie's sister, Sally. The other problem mentioned, which has not survived, but the content of which has been suggested by Professor Peter Heath, about two thieves and some apples, is given below. The answer, which was included in the letter, has been omitted.

> Tell Sally it's all very well to say she can do the two thieves and the [number omitted] apples, but can she do the fox and the goose and the bag of corn? That the man was bringing from market, and he had to get them over a river, and the boat was so tiny he could only take one across at a time; and he couldn't ever leave the fox and the goose together, for then the fox would eat the goose; and if he left the goose and the corn together, the goose would eat the corn. So the only things he could leave safely together were the fox and the corn, for you never see a fox eating corn, and you hardly ever see corn eating a fox. Ask her if she can do that puzzle?

This is a classic river-crossing problem. It was not invented by Lewis Carroll, but he often tried it out with friends.

The two thieves and apples problem goes like this:

> The first thief, finding a store of apples, stole half of them, plus half an apple. The second thief, coming after that, stole half of what the first thief stole, plus half an apple. There were then no apples left. How many apples were there in the first place?

## 27

# *The Thirty-Letter Game*

In a letter to a long-standing friend, Mrs. Winifred Hawke, which he wrote in January 1895, Lewis Carroll suggests a game, rather like Scrabble, for one or more players. The letter indicates that it is unlikely that he invented the game himself, but he does seem to have added his own rules. The letter reads:

> If ever you want a light mental recreation, try the "30 letter" puzzle. I tried it for the first time, the other day, with one of my sisters: and I think it very interesting. I have taught it to Enid, I think: but we have improved it. Here is our rule.
> "Take 4 or 5 complete alphabets. Put the vowels into one bag, the consonants into another. Shake up. Draw 9 vowels and 21 consonants. With these you must make 6 real words (excluding proper names) so as to use up all the letters. If two people want to do it, then after drawing a set of 30, pick out a set of duplicates for the other player. Sit where you cannot see one another's work, and make it a race. It seems to take from 5 to 10 minutes. It makes a shorter, but very good, puzzle, to draw 6 vowels and 14 consonants, and make 4 words; and a yet shorter one to draw 3 vowels and 7 consonants and make 2 words."

From *Sylvie and Bruno Concluded*:

> Here the kind-hearted Professor turned to the crowd and addressed them in a loud voice. "Learn your A's!" he shouted. "Your B's! Your C's! and your D's! Then you'll be at your ease!"

# The Square Window

In a letter to Helen Fielden which he wrote in March 1873, Lewis Carroll posed a problem about dealing with a square window that was giving too much light. Helen was fourteen at the time. In the letter, he goes on to relate an unfortunate incident in which the mother of a small girl totally spoils the fun of doing puzzles. The letter reads:

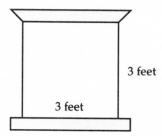

I don't know if you are fond of puzzles, or not. If you are, try this. If not, never mind. A gentleman (a nobleman let us say, to make it more interesting) had a sitting-room with only one window in it—a square window, 3 feet high and 3 feet wide. Now he had weak eyes, and the window gave too much light, so (don't you like "so" in a story?) he sent for the builder, and told him to alter it, so as to give half the light. Only, he was to keep it square—he was to keep it 3 feet high—and he was to keep it 3 feet wide. How did he do it? Remember, he wasn't allowed to use curtains, or shutters, or coloured glass, or anything of that sort.

I must tell you an awful story of my trying to set a puzzle to a little girl the other day. It was at a dinner party, at dessert. I had never seen her before, but, as she was sitting next me, I rashly proposed to her to try the puzzle (I daresay you know it) of "the fox, and goose, and bag of corn." And I got some biscuits to represent the fox and the other things. Her mother was sitting on the other side, and said, "Now mind you take pains, my dear, and do it right!" The consequences were awful! She shrieked out, "I can't do it! I can't do it! Oh, Mamma! Mamma!" threw herself into her mother's lap, and went off into a fit of sobbing which lasted several minutes! That was a lesson to me about trying children with puzzles. I do hope the square window won't produce any awful effect on you!

# The Three Squares

During a visit to Reading in August 1869, Lewis Carroll met Isabel Standen. He had been buying books from a shop which he had left to be collected later, and on his return to Guildford he realized that he had quite forgotten to pick up the books he had bought. He had been trying out a new puzzle with Isabel, and their meeting might have distracted his attention away from his purchases. However, in a letter to her the following day, he asks whether she would kindly go to the shop and ask for the books to be sent on. In the same letter he inquires whether or not Isabel had succeeded in drawing out the three-squares problem.

The three-squares problem is as follows:

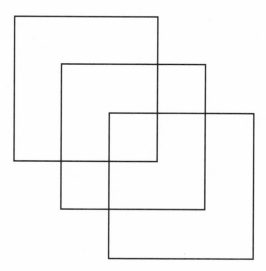

Draw these three interlaced squares without lifting your pencil from the paper, and without going over a line twice, *and* without intersecting any other line.

# *Doublets*

This game, invented by Lewis Carroll, appeared in issues of the magazine *Vanity Fair* between March 1879 and April 1881. He also published it as a booklet. This version was printed in 1879 and is a set of simpler rules, being an abridged version of the first issue. A later copy of the game, which came out in 1880, contains a method of scoring that is not included here.

> The rules of the Puzzle are simple enough. Two words are proposed, of the same length; and the Puzzle consists of linking these together by interposing other words, each of which shall differ from the next word *in one letter only*. That is to say, one letter may be changed in one of the given words, then one letter in the word so obtained, and so on, till we arrive at the other given word. The letters must not be interchanged among themselves, but each must keep to its own place. As an example, the word "head" may be changed into "tail" by interposing the words "heal, teal, tell, tall". I call the two given words "a Doublet", the interposed words "Links", and the entire series "a Chain", of which I here append an example:—

| H | E | A | D |
|---|---|---|---|
| h | e | a | l |
| t | e | a | l |
| t | e | l | l |
| t | a | l | l |
| T | A | I | L |

> It is, perhaps, needless to state that it is *de rigueur* that the links should be English words, such as might be used in good society.

The object is to complete a chain in the least number of links. Try these:

Drive PIG into STY

Raise FOUR to FIVE

# Diverse Doublets

The following doublets were published by Lewis Carroll as competition pieces in *Vanity Fair* from April through July 1879. See if you can complete chains for these doublets in the least number of links.

Cover EYE with LID

Prove PITY to be GOOD

Make EEL into PIE

Turn POOR into RICH

Prove RAVEN to be a MISER

Change OAT to RYE

Get WOOD from TREE

Prove GRASS to be GREEN

Evolve MAN from APE

Make FLOUR into BREAD

Run COMB into HAIR

Place BEANS on SHELF

Change BLACK to WHITE

Make KETTLE HOLDER

Turn WITCH into FAIRY

Make WINTER [into] SUMMER

Make BREAD into TOAST

If you want a real challenge, you might try driving HORSE into FIELD. In Lewis Carroll's day, the problem remained unsolved. In the last few years, the doublet has been accomplished using some modern words unknown in Victorian times.

# *Mischmasch*

Lewis Carroll invented this game for two players, and published it in *The Monthly Packet* in 1882. He also printed the rules, with slight variations, for circulation to his friends, and it is this version that is included here.

The essence of this game consists in one Player proposing a "nucleus" (i.e. a set of two or more letters, such as "gp", "emo", and "imse"), and in the other trying to find a "lawful word" (i.e. a word known in ordinary society, and not a proper name), containing it. Thus, "magpie", "lemon", "himself", are lawful words containing the nuclei "gp", "emo", "imse".

A nucleus must not contain a hyphen (e.g. for the nucleus "erga", "flower-garden" is not a lawful word).

Any word, that is always printed with a capital initial (e.g. "English"), counts as a proper name.

### RULES

1. Each thinks of a nucleus, and says "ready" when he has done so. When both have spoken, the nuclei are named. A Player may set a nucleus without knowing of any word containing it.

2. When a Player has guessed a word containing the nucleus set to him (which need not be the word thought of by the Player who set it), or has made up his mind that there is no such word, he says "ready", or "no word", as the case may be: when he has decided to give up trying, he says "I resign". The other must then, within a stated time (e.g. 2 minutes), say "ready", or "no word", or "I resign", or "not ready". If he says nothing, he is assumed to be "not ready".

3. When both have spoken, if the first speaker said "ready", he now names the word he has guessed: if he said "no word", he, who set the nucleus, names, if he can, a word containing it. The other Player then proceeds in the same way.

4. The Players then score as follows:—(N.B. When a Player is said to "lose" marks, it means that the other scores them.)

| | |
|---|---|
| Guessing a word, rightly, | scores 1. |
| Guessing a word, wrongly, | loses 1. |
| Guessing "no word", rightly, | scores 2. |
| Guessing "no word", wrongly, | loses 2. |
| Resigning | loses 1. |

This ends the first move.

5. For every other move, the Players proceed as for the first move, except that when a Player is "not ready", or has guessed a word wrongly, he has not a new nucleus set to him, but goes on guessing the one already in hand, having first, if necessary, set a new nucleus for the other Player.

6. A "resigned" nucleus cannot be set again during the same game. If, however, one or more letters be added or subtracted, it counts as a new one.

7. The move, in which either scores 10, is the final one; when it is completed, the game is over, and the highest score wins, or, if the scores be equal, the game is drawn.

# *Court Circular*

Lewis Carroll invented this card game for two players, and published it in 1862. It is based on a more complex game for two or more players which, according to his diary, he composed in 1858 and printed in 1860.

**First-Hand**

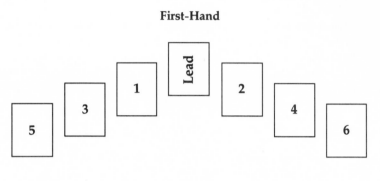

## I

Cut for deal; highest is "first-hand", lowest is dealer, and gives 6 cards to each, 3 at a time, turning up 13th as "Lead." First-hand then plays a card, then dealer, and so on, as numbered in the diagram, till 6 have been played, when the trick is complete. No. 5 is kept face down until No. 6 has been played.

## II

Whichever has, on his side of the trick, ("Lead" reckoning on each side,) the best "Line" of 3 cards, ("Lines" being of 3 kinds, which rank as follows: Trio, e.g. 3 Kings or 3 Nines; Sequence, e.g. Nine of Hearts, Eight of Spades, Seven of Hearts; Suit, e.g. 3 Diamonds) wins it. It does not matter in what order the cards have been played, (e.g. if "Lead" be Five of Hearts, and one of the players play Ace of Spaces, Seven of Clubs, Six of Diamonds, his side contains a Sequence). Trio containing "Lead" ranks above Trio not containing it, and so of Sequence and Suit. "Lead" must not be reckoned as the middle card of a Sequence. An Ace will form a Sequence with Two, Three, or with King, Queen.

## III

If equal Lines be made, he who has played, among the cards forming his Line, the best card, (cards ranking thus: Ace of Hearts, of Diamonds, of Clubs, of Spades, King of Hearts, etc.) wins the trick; if no Line be made, he who has played the best card wins it.

## IV

When the trick is won by superiority of Line, the winner adds the value of his own Line, (reckoned thus: Trio 1, Sequence 2, Suit 3,) to that of the loser's, if any, (reckoned thus: Trio 5, Sequence 3, Suit 1,) and takes so many cards; when by superiority of cards, he takes one only. Lead for the next trick is then chosen from the cards left on the table, (by the winner, if both or neither have made a Line; otherwise, by the loser,) and the others laid aside. The loser is dealer for the next trick, and gives 3 cards to each.

## V

When only 3 cards remain to be dealt, they are turned up, and each plays, either from the 3 cards in his hand, or from these 3, supplying its place from his own hand.

## VI

When the pack is out, every trick (after four) counts 1; most cards, 2; most court-cards, (Aces reckoning as court-cards,) 1. A Hit is 5, and two Hits make a Rubber.

# A Riddle

In Lewis Carroll's early magazine called *Mischmasch*, written between 1855 and 1862 for his three brothers and seven sisters, he included this verse-riddle. Can you discover the word to which it alludes?

> A monument—men all agree—
> Am I in all sincerity,
>   Half cat, half hindrance made.
> If head and tail removed should be,
> Then most of all you strengthen me;
> Replace my head, the stand you see
>   On which my tail is laid.

*Hint:*

> The table was a large one, but the three were all crowded together at one corner of it. "No room! No room!" they cried out when they saw Alice coming. "There's *plenty* of room!" said Alice indignantly, and she sat down in a large arm-chair at one end of the table.
>
> "Have some wine," the March Hare said in an encouraging tone.
>
> Alice looked all round the table, but there was nothing on it but tea. "I don't see any wine," she remarked.
>
> "There isn't any," said the March Hare.

—— 35 ——

# An Amazing Maze

In Lewis Carroll's family magazine called *Mischmasch*, he devised an amazing maze for his brothers and sisters to unravel. Can you find the way to the center?

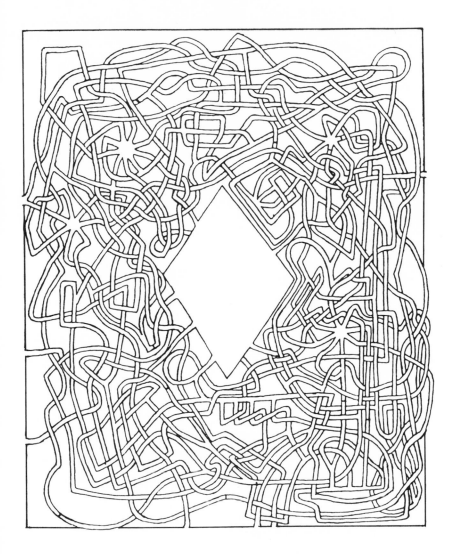

# A Convenient Number

*The Hunting of the Snark* is Lewis Carroll's epic nonsense poem. The idea, and the last line of the poem, came into his head while he was out walking near Guildford in July 1874. He completed nine verses four days later, which eventually became the last stanza of the poem. He continually added verses, finally writing the first stanza in January 1876. The whole poem was published later that year.

The fifth stanza contains this piece of mathematics which was proposed by the Butcher:

> Taking Three as the subject to reason about—
> A convenient number to state—
> We add Seven, and Ten, and then multiply out
> By One Thousand diminished by Eight.
>
> The result we proceed to divide, as you see,
> By Nine Hundred and Ninety and Two:
> Then subtract Seventeen, and the answer must be
> Exactly and perfectly true.

What is the answer?

Try the mathematics with other numbers. Why do you get these results?

--- **37** ---

# The Alphabet Cipher

This cipher was invented by Lewis Carroll, and published in 1868. In order to decode the message, a keyword is required. The table of letters, as given here, is also needed.

See if you can decode this extract. The method of decoding is left for you to discover.

"JNE ISN IOPI FXUST E UWM FSB HOV ES CAGUYLB?"
SBJH RHWEO, GW A IVVIU HQ MFJNHF XYA GWLHNCU.
"UIE DCWBQ CHF GMIOH FKW," BAJE XYA AQMI
CUSUPV: "JWPO RQE OFBK, WBF CM XN."
"XIEK W QWBGXUT QPRJ!" SZMJJINFH RHWEO.
"RQAU'T XYA FGKQXN UIIP'NS EKJUEE MIJOCPC,"
RQE HSCGDCP BCVASLIU: "XSEKSBE UIIP HSUCCW
FSPQ UWM VY BJY."

|   | A | B | C | D | E | F | G | H | I | J | K | L | M | N | O | P | Q | R | S | T | U | V | W | X | Y | Z |
|---|---|---|---|---|---|---|---|---|---|---|---|---|---|---|---|---|---|---|---|---|---|---|---|---|---|---|
| A | a | b | c | d | e | f | g | h | i | j | k | l | m | n | o | p | q | r | s | t | u | v | w | x | y | z |
| B | b | c | d | e | f | g | h | i | j | k | l | m | n | o | p | q | r | s | t | u | v | w | x | y | z | a |
| C | c | d | e | f | g | h | i | j | k | l | m | n | o | p | q | r | s | t | u | v | w | x | y | z | a | b |
| D | d | e | f | g | h | i | j | k | l | m | n | o | p | q | r | s | t | u | v | w | x | y | z | a | b | c |
| E | e | f | g | h | i | j | k | l | m | n | o | p | q | r | s | t | u | v | w | x | y | z | a | b | c | d |
| F | f | g | h | i | j | k | l | m | n | o | p | q | r | s | t | u | v | w | x | y | z | a | b | c | d | e |
| G | g | h | i | j | k | l | m | n | o | p | q | r | s | t | u | v | w | x | y | z | a | b | c | d | e | f |
| H | h | i | j | k | l | m | n | o | p | q | r | s | t | u | v | w | x | y | z | a | b | c | d | e | f | g |
| I | i | j | k | l | m | n | o | p | q | r | s | t | u | v | w | x | y | z | a | b | c | d | e | f | g | h |
| J | j | k | l | m | n | o | p | q | r | s | t | u | v | w | x | y | z | a | b | c | d | e | f | g | h | i |
| K | k | l | m | n | o | p | q | r | s | t | u | v | w | x | y | z | a | b | c | d | e | f | g | h | i | j |
| L | l | m | n | o | p | q | r | s | t | u | v | w | x | y | z | a | b | c | d | e | f | g | h | i | j | k |
| M | m | n | o | p | q | r | s | t | u | v | w | x | y | z | a | b | c | d | e | f | g | h | i | j | k | l |
| N | n | o | p | q | r | s | t | u | v | w | x | y | z | a | b | c | d | e | f | g | h | i | j | k | l | m |
| O | o | p | q | r | s | t | u | v | w | x | y | z | a | b | c | d | e | f | g | h | i | j | k | l | m | n |
| P | p | q | r | s | t | u | v | w | x | y | z | a | b | c | d | e | f | g | h | i | j | k | l | m | n | o |
| Q | q | r | s | t | u | v | w | x | y | z | a | b | c | d | e | f | g | h | i | j | k | l | m | n | o | p |
| R | r | s | t | u | v | w | x | y | z | a | b | c | d | e | f | g | h | i | j | k | l | m | n | o | p | q |
| S | s | t | u | v | w | x | y | z | a | b | c | d | e | f | g | h | i | j | k | l | m | n | o | p | q | r |
| T | t | u | v | w | x | y | z | a | b | c | d | e | f | g | h | i | j | k | l | m | n | o | p | q | r | s |
| U | u | v | w | x | y | z | a | b | c | d | e | f | g | h | i | j | k | l | m | n | o | p | q | r | s | t |
| V | v | w | x | y | z | a | b | c | d | e | f | g | h | i | j | k | l | m | n | o | p | q | r | s | t | u |
| W | w | x | y | z | a | b | c | d | e | f | g | h | i | j | k | l | m | n | o | p | q | r | s | t | u | v |
| X | x | y | z | a | b | c | d | e | f | g | h | i | j | k | l | m | n | o | p | q | r | s | t | u | v | w |
| Y | y | z | a | b | c | d | e | f | g | h | i | j | k | l | m | n | o | p | q | r | s | t | u | v | w | x |
| Z | z | a | b | c | d | e | f | g | h | i | j | k | l | m | n | o | p | q | r | s | t | u | v | w | x | y |

*Keyword hint:*

> "'Twas brillig, and the slithy toves
> Did gyre and gimble in the wabe"

# *Arithmetical Croquet*

Lewis Carroll made this entry in his diary for 24 October 1872:

> Wrote out, and sent to Gwendolen Cecil, the rules of a mental game I invented a short time ago, which I call Numerical Croquet.

The rules for this game, which become Arithmetical Croquet, were discovered written out by Lewis Carroll on a sheet dated April 22, 1889.

Try the game with a friend. See if you can play the game in your head. You may find this difficult at first, so try writing out your moves for a few initial games. Later, with practice you will become more accomplished, and will be able to play the game without paper.

### [RULES]

1. The first player names a number not greater than 8: the second does the same: the first then names a higher number, not advancing more than 8 beyond his last; and so on alternately—whoever names 100, which is "winning peg", wins the game.

2. The numbers 10, 20, etc. are the "hoops". To "take" a hoop, it is necessary to go, from a number below it, to one the same distance above it: e.g. to go from 17 to 23 would "take" the hoop 20: but to go to any other number above 20 would "miss it", in which case the player would have, in his next turn, to go back to a number below 20, in order to "take" it properly. To miss a hoop twice loses the game.

3. It is also lawful to "take" a hoop by playing *into* it, in one turn, and out of it, to the same distance above it in the next turn: e.g. to play from 17 to 20, and then from 20 to 23 in the next turn, would "take" the hoop 20. A player "in" a hoop may not play out of it with any other than the number so ordered.

4. Whatever step one player takes, bars the other from taking an equal step, or the difference between it and 9: e.g. if

one player advances 2, the other may not advance 2 or 7. But a player has no "barring" power when playing *into* a hoop, or when playing from any number between 90 and 100, unless the other player is also at such a number.

5. The "winning peg", like the "hoops", may be "missed" once, but to miss it twice loses the game.

6. When one player is "in" a hoop, the other can keep him in, by playing the number he needs for coming out, so as to bar him from using it. He can also do it by playing the difference between this and 9. And he may thus go on playing the 2 barring numbers alternately: but he may not play either twice running: e.g. if one player has gone from 17 to 20, the other can keep him in by playing 3, 6, 3, 6, etc.

"Can you play croquet?"

The soldiers were silent, and looked at Alice, as the question was evidently meant for her.

"Yes!" shouted Alice.

"Come on, then!" roared the Queen.

## — 39 —

# An Enigma

It is fairly certain that this puzzle was not invented by Lewis Carroll, but he did have copies made and circulated to his friends. He also prepared a solution sheet, and both were issued in 1866.
See if you can discover the answer to the riddle.

> I have a large Box, with two lids, two caps, three established Measures, and a great number of articles a Carpenter cannot do without.—Then I have always by me a couple of good Fish, and a number of a smaller tribe,—besides two lofty Trees, fine Flowers, and the fruit of an indigenous Plant; a handsome stag; two playful Animals; and a number of a smaller and less tame Herd:—Also two Halls, or Places of Worship; some Weapons of warfare; and many Weathercocks:—The Steps of an Hotel: The House of Commons on the eve of a Dissolution; Two Students or Scholars, and some Spanish Grandees, to wait upon me.
>
> All pronounce me a wonderful piece of Mechanism, but few have numbered up the strange medley of things which compose my whole.

"Have you guessed the riddle yet?" the Hatter said, turning to Alice again.

"No, I give it up," Alice replied. "What's the answer?"

"I haven't the slightest idea," said the Hatter.

"Nor I," said the March Hare.

# Square Numbers

Toward the end of his life, Lewis Carroll recorded in his diary that he had discovered that double the sum of two square numbers could always be written as the sum of two square numbers. A few days later, he realized that he had overlooked a piece of elementary algebra that proved this result.

Here are some examples:

$$2(3^2 + 4^2) = 2(9 + 16) = 50 = 1 + 49 = 1^2 + 7^2$$
$$2(5^2 + 8^2) = 2(25 + 64) = 178 = 9 + 169 = 3^2 + 13^2$$

Try some of your own examples.

See if you can prove this result for double any two square numbers.

In his book *Pillow-Problems*, he extends this idea with this problem:

Prove that 3 times the sum of 3 squares is also the sum of 4 squares.

Again, try some examples first, and then see if you can work out an algebraic proof.

"I only took the regular course."

"What was that?" inquired Alice.

"Reeling and Writhing, of course, to begin with," the Mock Turtle replied; "and then the different branches of Arithmetic—Ambition, Distraction, Uglification, and Derision."

"I never heard of 'Uglification'," Alice ventured to say. "What is it?"

The Gryphon lifted up both its paws in surprise. "Never heard of uglifying!" it exclaimed. "You know what to beautify is, I suppose?"

"Yes," said Alice doubtfully: "it means—to—make—any-thing—prettier."

"Well, then," the Gryphon went on, "if you don't know what to uglify is, you *are* a simpleton."

— 41 —

# *Carrollian Cross Reference*

A cross reference puzzle is like a crossword without clues. The numbers represent the 26 letters of the alphabet. In this puzzle, the numbers 1, 15 and 7 represent the letters W, I and T respectively. Begin by repeating these letters wherever 1, 15 and 7 occur in the diagram. You will then have some clues to the rest of the missing words. Remember that many of the words are linked to Lewis Carroll's books. When completed, the diagram looks like an ordinary crossword puzzle.

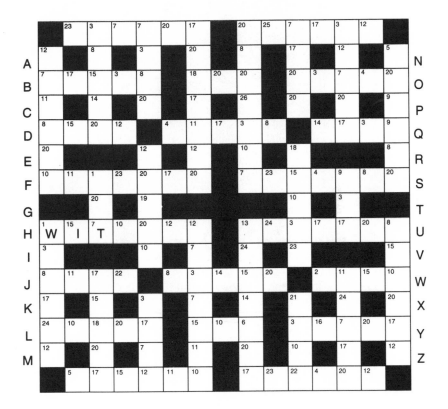

REFERENCE GRID

| 1 W | 2 | 3 | 4 | 5 | 6 | 7 T | 8 | 9 | 10 | 11 | 12 | 13 |
|---|---|---|---|---|---|---|---|---|---|---|---|---|
| 14 | 15 I | 16 | 17 | 18 | 19 | 20 | 21 | 22 | 23 | 24 | 25 | 26 |

57

—— **42** ——

# The Number Forty-Two

There is little doubt that Lewis Carroll had a certain fascination with the number forty-two; he often used this number in his writings:

> At this moment the King, who had been for some time busily writing in his note-book, called out "Silence!" and read out from his book "Rule Forty-Two. *All persons more than a mile high to leave the court.*" [From *Alice's Adventures in Wonderland*, which, incidentally, has 42 illustrations.]

> "Four thousand two hundred and seven, that's the exact number," the King said, referring to his book. "I couldn't send all the horses, you know, because two of them are wanted in the game." [From *Through the Looking-Glass*, which was originally planned to have 42 illustrations; in the end there were 50.]

> > "No doubt", said I, "they settled who
> >     Was fittest to be sent:
> > Yet still to choose a brat like you,
> > To haunt a man of forty-two,
> >     Was no great compliment!"
>
> > [From *Phantasmagoria*.]

The helmsman used to stand by with tears in his eyes: *he* knew it was all wrong, but alas! Rule 42 of the Code, *"No one shall speak to the Man at the Helm,"* had been completed by the Bellman himself with the words *"and the Man at the Helm shall speak to no one."*

> He had forty-two boxes, all carefully packed,
> With his name painted clearly on each:
> But, since he omitted to mention the fact,
> They were all left behind on the beach.

[From *The Hunting of the Snark.*]

There are other references to the number forty-two, some disguised to make his use of the number less obvious. For example: just before the Queen's croquet match in *Alice's Adventures in Wonderland*, three playing cards are busily painting the roses red. These cards are numbered 2, 5 and 7; these are all prime numbers. Their sum is 14. The missing number in the prime sequence is 3. Multiplying 14 by 3 gives 42.

Now, here is your chance to discover the number forty-two hidden in *Through the Looking-Glass:*

> "Let's consider your age to begin with——how old are you?
> "I'm seven and a half, exactly."
> "You needn't say 'exactually,'" the Queen remarked: "I can believe it without that. Now I'll give *you* something to believe. I'm just one hundred and one, five months and a day."
> "I ca'n't believe *that!*" said Alice.

Alice Liddell's birthday was on May 4, 1852.
Hence, at this moment in the story, it was November 4, 1859.
The following year, 1860, was a leap year (366 days).
The White Queen and her counterpart, the Red Queen, had each lived for 101 years, 5 months and 1 day.
The five months must be June through to October.
From the information given, their birthday was June 3, 1758.

How many days in total had the two Queens lived?
How is this connected with the number 42?

# The Solutions to
# the Puzzles

## 1. *Cakes in a Row*

One possible solution is:

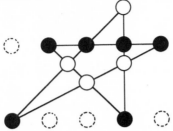

Other solutions use the possibility of stacking cakes on top of each other.

## 2. *More Cakes in a Row*

(1)

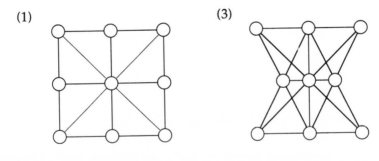

(3)

(2)

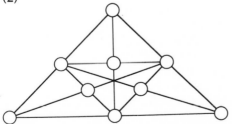

## 3. *On the Top of a High Wall*

Ten apples appeared. (Second line: "And dreaming of-ten, dear.")

## 4. *A Sticky Problem*

Just less than 4 ounces each; don't forget that the sawdust is lost!

## 5. *Two Brothers and a Box*

This solution, slightly modified here, appeared in the January 1871 issue of *Aunt Judy's Magazine*. The verse was not written by Lewis Carroll, but by "Eadgyth," which is probably the pen name for either the editor of the magazine or one of her family. This issue of the magazine was edited by Mrs. Gatty, with contributions by her son and daughter.

> As curly-headed James was sleeping in bed,
> His brother John gave him a blow on the head;
> James opened his eyelids, and spying his brother,
> Doubled his fist, and gave him another.
> This kind of box then is not so rare;
> The lids are the eyelids, the locks are the hair,
> And so every schoolboy can tell to his cost,
> The key to the tangles is constantly lost.

## 6. *Wise Eyes*

Sixteen wise men still trouble the land.

## 7. *Alice's Multiplication Tables*

$$4 \times 5 = 12 \quad \text{(20 in base 18)}$$
$$4 \times 6 = 13 \quad \text{(24 in base 21)}$$
$$4 \times 7 = 14 \quad \text{(28 in base 24)}$$
$$4 \times 8 = 15 \quad \text{(32 in base 27)}$$
$$4 \times 9 = 16 \quad \text{(36 in base 30)}$$
$$4 \times 10 = 17 \quad \text{(40 in base 33)}$$
$$4 \times 11 = 18 \quad \text{(44 in base 36)}$$
$$4 \times 12 = 19 \quad \text{(48 in base 39)}$$
$$4 \times 13 = 20 \quad \text{(not 52 in base 42)}$$

1T would be 52 in base 42.

It has also been suggested that children learn tables up to "12 times," and hence Alice would not reach 20 in this manner.

## 8. *Magic Postal Square*

The 4d stamp is used twice. On one square, the $\frac{1}{2}$d stamp and one of the 4d stamps are placed. The Postal Square when completed looks like this:

| $2\frac{1}{2}$d | 5d | $1\frac{1}{2}$d |
|---|---|---|
| 2d | 3d | 4d |
| $4\frac{1}{2}$d | 1d | $3\frac{1}{2}$d |

## 9. *Who's Telling the Truth?*

The Hatter is telling the truth.

The Dodo lies when he says that the Hatter is lying. The Hatter is telling the truth when he says that the March Hare is lying. The March Hare is lying when he says both the Dodo and the Hatter are lying since one is telling the truth.

## 11. *Russian Family*

Yvan is the name of the youngest son.

Rab became a lawyer; he went to the BAR.
Ymra became a soldier; he joined the ARMY.
The youngest, if he became a sailor, joined the NAVY; hence YVAN.

## 12. *Fair Shares*

£80 was divided between them in the following stages:

| Elder | Younger |
|---|---|
| £42 | £38 |
| £28 | £52 |
| £54 | £26 |
| £18 | £62 |
| £64.50 | £15.50 |
| £21.50 | £58.50 |
| £41 | £39 |
| £40 | £40 |

## 13. *A Mysterious Number*

The number is the first six decimal places of one-seventh written as a whole number. These six figures recur in the decimal. One-seventh multiplied by 7 gives 1, or 0.999999, bearing in mind the error caused by limiting the number to only six decimal places.

## 14. *Looking-Glass Time*

Approximately 27 minutes 42 seconds past 6 o'clock ($27\frac{9}{13}$ minutes to be precise).

At six o'clock the minute hand and the hour hand are exactly 180° apart. Let the hour hand move through $x°$. Then, if the time is reversible in a mirror, the minute hand has moved through $(180 - x)°$. The hour hand moves at 30° per hour. The minute hand moves at 360° per hour. The time elapsed during which both hands move is identical. It follows that:

$$\frac{180 - x}{360} = \frac{x}{30}$$

$$x = \frac{180}{13}$$

Hence, this angle represents $\dfrac{180}{13} \times \dfrac{1}{360} \times 60$ minutes on the clock face. This reduces to $2\frac{4}{13}$ minutes.

Hence the time is $30 - 2\frac{4}{13}$ minutes past 6 o'clock; i.e., $27\frac{9}{13}$ minutes past 6 o'clock.

## 15. *Painting Cubes*

Thirty differently painted cubes.

Let the six faces be *a, b, c, d, e* and *f*. With face *a* opposite face *b*, there are six arrangements for the other four colors around the cube: *cdef, cdfe, cedf, cefd, cfde* and *cfed*. Likewise for face *a* opposite face *c*; face *a* opposite face *d*; face *a* opposite face *e*; face *a* opposite face *f*; all have six arrangements for the remaining four colors. Hence the total is $5 \times 6 = 30$ arrangements.

## 16. *Going Out*

This is Lewis Carroll's solution:

> Let "Q is R" mean "A & B go out";
> "H is K" mean "A, B & C go out";
> "X is Y" mean "C, D & E go out".
> Then the 2 rules may be expressed
> thus:
> (1) If H is K, F must stay in;
> (2) If X is Y, F must go out.
> Hence (3), If X is Y, H cannot be K.

If possible, let A & B be supposed to go out together; i.e. if possible, let Q be R.

Now, if we assume "Q is R", the condition "X is Y" involves the condition "H is K"; i.e. if Q is R, the Proposition "if X is Y, then H is K" is true; but by (3), it cannot be true.

Therefore "Q is R" cannot be true; i.e. A & B cannot go out together.

It has been pointed out to me by Mark Richards, who has made a study of Carroll's logic, that there is an error in this solution. This is, in fact, the famous barbershop logical problem, and it may be converted to this form:

> Let L mean X is Y
> M mean H cannot be K
> and N mean Q is R

Then we have by (3): If L is true, then M is true; and: If N is true then the proposition "If L is true, then M is not true" is true [as stated in the solution given above].

In fact Carroll's view in all subsequent solutions states that N can be true, i.e. Q can be R, i.e. A and B can go out together. Carroll's logical rival at Oxford, the Professor of Logic, John Cook-Wilson, believed that A and B could not go out together.

Hence it is likely that this solution, in Carroll's hand, was an early attempt at solving the problem which he later revised.

## 17. *Four Brothers and a Monkey*

There were 765 nuts on the table.

1st Brother:
$$765 - 1 = 764 = 4 \times 191$$
$$3 \times 191 = 573$$

2nd Brother:
$$573 - 1 = 572 = 4 \times 143$$
$$3 \times 143 = 429$$

3rd Brother:
$$429 - 1 = 428 = 4 \times 107$$
$$3 \times 107 = 321$$

4th Brother:
$$321 - 1 = 320 = 4 \times 80$$
$$3 \times \phantom{0}80 = 240$$

Remaining nuts: $240 = 4 \times 60$.

Other solutions: 2813, 5885.

## 18. *Two Clocks*

The clock that is right only once a year is the better one; the other has stopped.

## 19. *Sitting in a Circle*

Here is Lewis Carroll's solution given in *Pillow-Problems* (modified to fit today's currency):

Let $m$ = number of men, $k$ = number of pounds possessed by the last (i.e. the poorest) man. After one circuit, each is a pound poorer, and the moving heap contains $m$ pounds. Hence, after $k$ circuits, each is $k$ pounds poorer, the last man now having nothing, and the moving heap contains $mk$ pounds. Hence the thing ends when the last man is again called on to hand on the heap, which then contains $(mk + m - 1)$ pounds, the penultimate man now having nothing, and the first man having $(m - 2)$ pounds.

It is evident that the first and the last man are the only 2 neighbours whose possessions can be in the ratio "4 to 1". Hence either

$$mk + m - 1 = 4(m - 2),$$
or else $\quad 4(mk + m - 1) = m - 2.$

The first equation gives $mk = 3m - 7$, i.e. $k = 3 - \frac{7}{m}$, which evidently gives no integral values other than $m = 7$, $k = 2$.

The second gives $4mk = 2 - 3m$, which evidently gives no positive integral values.

Hence the answer is 7 men; 2 pounds.

## 20. *Bags of Counters*

Here are Lewis Carroll's solutions from *Pillow-Problems:*

*Problem Number 5*

At first sight, it would appear that, as the state of the bag, *after* the operation, is necessarily identical with its state *before it*, the chance is just what it then was, viz. $\frac{1}{2}$. This, however, is an error.

The chances, *before* the addition, that the bag contains (a) 1 white (b) 1 black, are (a) $\frac{1}{2}$ (b) $\frac{1}{2}$. Hence the chances, *after* the addition, that it contains (a) 2 white (b) 1 white, 1 black, are the same, viz. (a) $\frac{1}{2}$ (b) $\frac{1}{2}$. Now the probabilities, which these 2 states give to the observed event, of drawing a white counter, are (a) certainty (b) $\frac{1}{2}$. Hence the chances, after drawing the white counter, that the bag, before drawing, contained (a) 2 white (b) 1 white, 1 black, are proportional to (a) $\frac{1}{2}$ [to] 1 (b) $\frac{1}{2}$ [to] $\frac{1}{2}$, i.e. (a) $\frac{1}{2}$ (b) $\frac{1}{4}$, i.e. (a) 2 (b) 1. Hence the chances are (a) $\frac{2}{3}$ (b) $\frac{1}{3}$. Hence, after the removal of a white counter, the chances, that the bag now contains (a) 1 white (b) 1 black, are for (a) $\frac{2}{3}$ and for (b) $\frac{1}{3}$.

Thus the chance, of now drawing a white counter, is $\frac{2}{3}$.

*Problem Number 16*

The "a priori" chances of possible states of first bag are "$W, \frac{1}{2}$; $B, \frac{1}{2}$". Hence chances, after putting $W$ in, are "$WW, \frac{1}{2}$; $WB, \frac{1}{2}$". The chances, which these give to the "observed event", are $1, \frac{1}{2}$. Hence chances of possible states "$W, B$", after the event, are proportional to $1, \frac{1}{2}$; i.e. to $2, 1$; i.e. their actual values are $\frac{2}{3}, \frac{1}{3}$.

Now, in first course, chance of drawing $W$ is $\frac{1}{2} \cdot \frac{2}{3} + \frac{1}{2} \cdot \frac{1}{3}$; i.e. $\frac{1}{2}$. And, in second course, chances of possible states "$WWBB$, $WBBB$" are $\frac{2}{3}, \frac{1}{3}$; hence chance of drawing $W$ is $\frac{2}{3} \cdot \frac{1}{2} + \frac{1}{3} \cdot \frac{1}{4}$; i.e. $\frac{5}{12}$. Hence *first* course gives best chance.

*Problem Number 72*

We know that, if a bag contained 3 counters, 2 being black and one white, the chance of drawing a black one would be $\frac{2}{3}$; and that any *other* state of things would *not* give this chance.

Now the chances, that the given bag contains $(\alpha)$ $BB$, $(\beta)$ $BW$, $(\gamma)$ $WW$, are respectively $\frac{1}{4}, \frac{1}{2}, \frac{1}{4}$.

Add a black counter.

Then the chances, that it contains $(\alpha)$ $BBB$, $(\beta)$ $BWB$, $(\gamma)$ $WWB$, are, as before, $\frac{1}{4}, \frac{1}{2}, \frac{1}{4}$.

Hence the chance, of now drawing a black one,

$$= \frac{1}{4} \cdot 1 + \frac{1}{2} \cdot \frac{2}{3} + \frac{1}{4} \cdot \frac{1}{3} = \frac{2}{3}.$$

Hence the bag now contains $BBW$ (since any *other* state of things would *not* give this chance).

Hence, before the black counter was added, it contained $BW$, i.e. one black counter and one white.

(An interesting proof, which needs careful scrutiny; there is an element of "tongue-in-cheek" with this result.)

## 21. *Going Round in Circles*

They can all be drawn in one line following Lewis Carroll's specific rule, but care must be taken in deciding which direction to take at a point of contact with a new circle or oval. As a general strategy, if you start on an outer circle and alternate the directions left and right at each new contact point, you will find that it is quite easy to draw these networks. The path for diagram 3 is given below:

Start

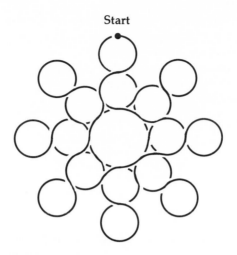

## 22. *Hidden Names*

The first letter of each line gives:

ALICE PLEASANCE LIDDELL

## 23. *Another Hidden Name*

The first letter of each line, and the first word of each verse, gives:

GERTRUDE CHATAWAY

## 24. *Well-Hidden Names*

The third letter of each line gives:

ENID STEVENS

The second letter of each line gives:

CLIMENE MARY HOLIDAY

## 25. *Handicaps*

Runner A requires a 44-yard start, and runner C requires a 40-yard handicap.

## 26. *The Fox, the Goose and the Bag of Corn*

> Take goose across river.
> Return.
> Take fox across river.
> Return with goose.
> Take corn across river, leaving goose behind.
> Return.
> Take goose across river.

Five apples were in the store.

## 28. *The Square Window*

The window was reduced in size as the following diagram illustrates:

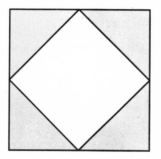

## 29. *The Three Squares*

A path showing how to draw this network is shown in the diagram below (there are other possible solutions):

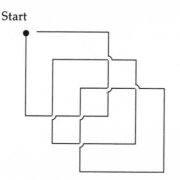

## 30. Doublets

| | |
|---|---|
| P I G | F O U R |
| w i g | f o u l |
| w a g | f o o l |
| w a y | f o o t |
| s a y | f o r t |
| S T Y | f o r e |
| | f i r e |
| | F I V E |

## 31. Diverse Doublets

| | | | |
|---|---|---|---|
| E Y E | P I T Y | E E L | P O O R |
| d y e | p i t s | e e n | b o o r |
| d i e | p i n s | p e n | b o o k |
| d i d | f i n s | p i n | r o o k |
| L I D | f i n d | P I E | r o c k |
| | f o n d | | r i c k |
| | f o o d | | R I C H |
| | G O O D | | |

| | | | |
|---|---|---|---|
| R A V E N | O A T | T R E E | G R A S S |
| r i v e n | r a t | f r e e | c r a s s |
| r i s e n | r o t | f l e e | c r e s s |
| r i s e r | r o e | f l e d | t r e s s |
| M I S E R | R Y E | f e e d | t r e e s |
| | | w e e d | f r e e s |
| | | w e l d | f r e e d |
| | | w o l d | g r e e d |
| | | W O O D | G R E E N |

| | | | |
|---|---|---|---|
| A P E | F L O U R | C O M B | B E A N S |
| a r e | f l o o r | c o m e | b e a m s |
| e r e | f l o o d | h o m e | s e a m s |
| e r r | b l o o d | h o l e | s h a m s |
| e a r | b r o o d | h a l e | s h a m e |
| m a r | b r o a d | h a l l | s h a l e |
| M A N | B R E A D | h a i l | s h a l l |
| | | H A I R | s h e l l |
| | | | S H E L F |

```
BLACK        KETTLE       WITCH
blank        settle       winch
blink        settee       wench
clink        setter       tench
chink        better       tenth
chine        betted       tents
whine        belted       tints
WHITE        bolted       tilts
             bolter       tills
             bolder       fills
             HOLDER       falls
                          fails
                          fairs
                          FAIRY

WINTER       BREAD
winner       break
wanner       bleak
wander       bleat
warder       blest
harder       blast
harper       boast
hamper       TOAST
damper
damped
dammed
dimmed
dimmer
simmer
SUMMER
```

## 34. *A Riddle*

Tablet.

## 35. *An Amazing Maze*

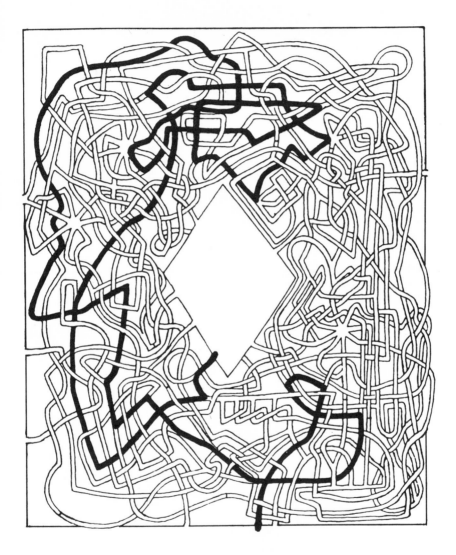

## 36. *A Convenient Number*

Three.

The second verse reverses the arithmetical operations in the first verse, so that any number chosen, except minus seventeen, would remain unchanged.

## 37. *The Alphabet Cipher*

Keyword: "Jabberwocky"
Message:

> "And how many hours a day did you do lessons?" said Alice, in a hurry to change the subject.
> "Ten hours the first day," said the Mock Turtle: "nine the next, and so on."
> "What a curious plan!" exclaimed Alice.
> "That's the reason they're called lessons," the Gryphon remarked: "because they lessen from day to day."

Method:

```
Keyword:  J A B B E R W O C K Y J A B B E R ...
Message:  A N D H O W M A N Y H O U R S A D ...
Code:     J N E I S N I O P I F X U S T E U ...
```

## 39. *An Enigma*

Here is Lewis Carroll's explication of the Enigma:

The Whole—is Man.

The Parts are as follows.

A large Box—The Chest.
Two lids—The Eye lids.
Two Caps—The Knee Caps.
Three established Measures—The nails, hands and feet.
A great number of articles a Carpenter cannot do without,— Nails.
A couple of good Fish—The Soles of the Feet.
A number of a smaller tribe—The Muscles (Mussels).
Two lofty Trees—The Palms (of the hands).

Fine Flowers—Two lips, (Tulips), and Irises.

The fruit of an indigenous Plant—Hips.

A handsome Stag—The Heart. (Hart).

Two playful Animals—The Calves.

A number of a smaller and less tame Herd—The Hairs. (Hares).

Two Halls, or Places of Worship—The Temples.

Some Weapons of Warfare—The Arms, and Shoulder blades.

Many Weathercocks—The Veins. (Vanes).

The Steps of an Hotel—The Insteps. (Inn-steps).

The House of Commons on the eve of a Dissolution—Eyes and Nose. (Ayes and Noes).

Two Students or Scholars—The Pupils of the Eye.

Some Spanish Grandees—The Tendons. (Ten Dons).

## 40. *Square Numbers*

$$2(a^2 + b^2) = (a - b)^2 + (a + b)^2$$

$$3(a^2 + b^2 + c^2) = (a + b + c)^2 + (b - c)^2 + (c - a)^2 + (a - b)^2$$

## 41. *Carrollian Cross Reference*

## 42. *The Number Forty-Two*

The Queens are 101 years, 5 months and 1 day old.

In total, the number of days they have lived is calculated as follows:

101 years (which includes 25 leap years)

non-leap years $76 \times 365 = 27740$ days
leap years $25 \times 366 = \phantom{0}9150$ days
Total for 101 years: $\phantom{00}36890$ days

The five months are from June 4 to November 3 (inclusive):

| | |
|---|---|
| rest of June | 27 days |
| July | 31 days |
| August | 31 days |
| September | 30 days |
| October | 31 days |
| start of November | 3 days |
| | Total: 153 days |

Total for both Queens:

| | | |
|---|---|---|
| Years: | 36890 days | (Red Queen) |
| | 36890 days | (White Queen) |
| Months: | 153 days | (RQ) |
| | 153 days | (WQ) |
| Extra day: | 1 day | (RQ) |
| | 1 day | (WQ) |
| Grand total: | 74088 days | |

This is exactly $42 \times 42 \times 42$.

# Sources

*The Diaries of Lewis Carroll,* edited by Roger Lancelyn Green; published by Cassell in 1954.

"Further Findings about the Number Forty Two," by Edward Wakeling; printed in *Jabberwocky, The Journal of the Lewis Carroll Society,* Vol. 17, Joint Nos. 1 and 2, in 1988.

*The Letters of Lewis Carroll,* edited by Morton Cohen with the assistance of Roger Lancelyn Green; published by Macmillan in 1979.

"Lewis Carroll et le Nombre 42," by Edward Wakeling; printed in *Europe: Revue Littéraire Mensuelle,* August/September 1990.

*The Lewis Carroll Handbook,* revised edition by Denis Crutch; published by Dawson Archon in 1979.

*The Lewis Carroll Circulars: Numbers 1 and 2,* edited by Trevor Winkfield; privately published in 1973 and 1974 respectively.

*The Magic of Lewis Carroll,* edited by John Fisher; published by Nelson in 1973.

*Professor Bartholomew Price, Mathematics Tutor and Charles Dodgson (Lewis Carroll), His Pupil,* by Edward Wakeling; privately published in 1980.

"What I Tell You Forty-Two Times is True!" by Edward Wakeling; printed in *Jabberwocky, The Journal of the Lewis Carroll Society,* Vol. 6, No. 4, in 1977.

## THE WORKS OF LEWIS CARROLL

*The Rectory Umbrella* (1850–53)
*Mischmasch* (1855–62)
"The Rules for Court Circular" (1862)
*Alice's Adventures in Wonderland* (1865)
"Enigma" (1866)
"Explication of the Enigma" (1866)
"The Alphabet Cipher" (1868)
*Phantasmagoria* (1869)
"Puzzles from Wonderland" (1870)

*Through the Looking-Glass* (1871)
*The Hunting of the Snark* (1876)
"Lanrick" (1878)
*Doublets* (1879)
"Mischmasch" (1882)
"Arithmetical Croquet" (1889)
*Sylvie and Bruno* (1889)
*Pillow-Problems* (1893)
*Sylvie and Bruno Concluded* (1893)
"A Mysterious Number" (1897)